How can I be sure?

And other questions about doubt, assurance and the Bible

John Stevens

Questions Christians ask

How can I be sure?
And other questions about doubt, assurance and the Bible
© John Stevens/The Good Book Company, 2014
Reprinted 2015

Published by
The Good Book Company
Tel (UK): 0333 123 0880
Tel (North America): (1) 866 244 2165
International: +44 (0) 208 942 0880
Email (UK): info@thegoodbook.co.uk
Email (North America): info@thegoodbook.com

Websites
UK & Europe: www.thegoodbook.co.uk
North America: www.thegoodbook.com
Australia: www.thegoodbook.com.au
New Zealand: www.thegoodbook.co.nz

ISBN: 9781909559158

Printed in the UK by CPI Group (UK) Ltd, Croydon, CR0 4YY
Design by André Parker

Contents

The problem of doubt

I became a Christian in 1988 while I was a law student. I had grown up in a non-Christian family, and started university as a convinced atheist. I became a Christian through the witness of a number of friends from my course, who shared the good news about Jesus with me and invited me to numerous evangelistic meetings. I resisted God's call on my life for more than a year, but finally trusted in Christ at the beginning of my final year.

Given that I had already had to overcome my scepticism and unbelief to become a Christian, I started out with a confident faith in Jesus. I was conscious of growing in faith and enjoying a new relationship with God. However, over the years I found that I had to face new doubts. I continued to struggle with sin and was frustrated by my failures. Sometimes God felt distant and I wondered whether my relationship with him was real. I discovered new theological and philosophical challenges to my faith and the truthfulness of the Bible. I felt the frustrations of seeing little fruit from my ministry and the disappointments of being let down by church and other Christians.

Five years after I had become a Christian, my father died from lung cancer without ever, to my knowledge, professing faith in Christ. Watching him die painfully and slowly inevitably made me question my faith in a new way. How could a God of love allow such a slow, painful and lingering death? Was it really possible to believe in a bodily resurrection? Would a loving God really send those who had rejected Jesus to eternal punishment in Hell for ever? I had faced some of these questions intellectually, and knew what the Bible said, but my experience meant that I now faced them in a different way. They were no longer abstract questions of moral philosophy but bound up with the loss of someone I had loved. It took me several years to recover a confident and assured faith after the anguish of this time.

I have now been involved in church leadership for almost twenty years. During that time I have had the privilege of ministering to all different kinds of people, at all stages of life. I have spent time with many who have struggled with doubts, or a lack of assurance about their salvation. Some have struggled with intense and long-lasting doubt and they have endured a real fight to keep their faith. Whether a period of doubt is short or long, it usually robs Christians of their joy, peace and delight in God, and prevents them serving him wholeheartedly and sacrificially. It turns them inwards as they search their hearts and consciences for signs of real faith, and may cause them paralysing fear as to whether they are believers at all.

Doubt is one of the hidden struggles that many Christians face. Christians know that they are meant to be people of "faith", and so they find it hard to admit that they are struggling with doubt. You may fear that other Christians will respect you less, stop you from serving in ministry, or even withdraw their friendship. However, it is vital that we are honest about the problem, so that we can find help and recover a joyful and confident faith.

You may be reading this because you are struggling with doubt yourself, or because you know others who are struggling. My prayer is that you will be reassured to discover that doubt is a common experience for God's people, and that you will be helped to grow stronger in your faith.

There is no single reason why Christians experience doubt. The following fictional cases, drawn from my pastoral experiences, show how some Christians have come to doubt.

Aidan

Aidan is a committed Christian in his twenties. He has long struggled with an addiction to internet pornography. Much of the time he is able to resist his desire, but then he is gripped by an irresistible urge to download again. This often happens when he is feeling low, lonely or unhappy. These repeated failures make him feel that he cannot really be a true believer. How can he be forgiven and indwelt by the Holy Spirit when he keeps failing and falling in this way?

Barbara

Barbara is a retired missionary who spent many years serving the Lord in South America. Shortly after she arrived back, she was diagnosed with aggressive breast cancer. Many friends around the world have been praying for her to be healed, but these prayers have not been answered. She is questioning whether there can be a good and loving God if he has allowed her to become ill like this after a lifetime of faithful service.

Catherine

Catherine is in her early thirties. She became a Christian through an Alpha course. She has struggled with depression and is resentful that she is still single. Recently a new Muslim colleague joined her team at work. She finds him attractive and he has asked her out on a date. Although he attends Mosque regularly, he says that he thinks that all religions are the same. She has started to wonder whether it can be really true that Jesus is the only way to God.

Dan

Dan cannot remember a time when he did not believe in Jesus. His family taught him from an early age that the Bible is true and trustworthy. He is now studying engineering at university and has become good friends with a theology student. This friend has told him that the Bible is full of errors and contradictions, and has lent him some books. He is beginning to wonder if he can really trust the Bible and keep believing in Jesus.

Ellie

Ellie became a Christian on a summer camp with her best friend from school. She is now the president of the Christian Union at her university. Her older brother recently came out as gay. He has found a partner and they are planning to marry. Ellie can see that her brother loves his partner very much, and that he is happier in this relationship than he has ever been. She is finding it hard to believe in a God who would condemn her brother's relationship. How can her faith be true if this is what it requires?

Femi

Femi is from a Nigerian family and grew up in a large Pentecostal church. He became a Christian after a dramatic conversion experience which included an overpowering sense of the love and presence of God, and speaking in tongues. However, he has not felt close to God for the past few months, and he is beginning to wonder whether his conversion was ever real. He has stopped going to church because he doesn't seem to "get" anything out of it.

Graham

Graham has been a Christian for more than twenty years. He has never experienced any significant periods when he has questioned his faith, but he is troubled that he occasionally finds himself wondering, for no apparent reason, whether what he believes can really be true, especially when the vast majority of other people aren't Christians. These times pass quickly as he reminds himself of the facts of the gospel, but he can't help but wonder if there is something fundamentally wrong with his faith.

Jennifer

Jennifer grew up in a strong Christian family. She cannot remember a time that she did not believe in Jesus and pray to him. She is very active in her local church. She doesn't question the truth of the Christian faith, but deep down she is anxious about whether she is really a Christian herself. She hasn't had a dramatic conversion experience like some of her friends, and wouldn't say that she had ever had any deep sense of conviction of sin or passionate delight in her salvation. Most of the time she is happy and content, but she wonders if she really has true spiritual life.

The good news is that even if Christians and churches tend not to be open and honest about doubt, the Bible faces the problem of doubt head on. It admits that doubt will be a problem for all of God's people for some of the time, and for some of God's people for much of the time.

The most famous doubter in the Bible is the apostle Thomas. John's Gospel tells how Thomas first refused to believe that Jesus had really risen, even though he had appeared to the other disciples. Thomas told them: "Unless I see the nail marks in his hands and put my finger where the nails were, and put my hand into his side, I will not believe" (John 20 v 25). Jesus appeared again a week later, only this time Thomas was with the other disciples. When he saw Jesus he proclaimed: "My Lord and my God!" (John 20 v 28).

Many who struggle with doubt hunger for an experience like this. But Jesus doesn't promise it—quite the opposite. He has spoken to us through his word, and this is sufficient. When Thomas finally believed, Jesus did not commend him for his faith, but told him:

> Because you have seen me, you have believed;
> blessed are those who have not seen and yet have
> believed.   *John 20 v 29*

Jesus does not promise us that we will "see" in this life. We are called to "live by faith" in the promise of his word, not by sight. The word we have in the Bible is completely sufficient to meet the challenge of doubts. In the rest of this book we will listen to what God has to say to us in the Scriptures so that we can have confident faith in the Lord Jesus.

"The art of doubting is easy, for it is an ability that is born with us."
Martin Luther

Chapter 1

What is doubt?

What do we mean by doubt? Doubt is a word that has a wide range of meanings. The Bible rarely uses the term, although it speaks much about faith and belief. We use "doubt" to describe a number of different feelings of uncertainty, not all of which are equally serious spiritual problems.

Doubt as uncertainty about the future

At the most basic level we use "doubt" to mean the opposite of "certainty". If asked whether it is going to rain today, someone might reply: "I doubt it". Such doubt is not always a bad thing. I am right to doubt my child's promise that she won't go near the cliff edge, or the con-man's claim that he will double my money. And I ought to doubt that an England team will win any international sporting competition.

Here "doubt" describes a lack of certainty about an

unpredictable outcome, and expresses our judgement that a particular possibility is unlikely. Christians may often suffer from doubt of this kind, as for example where they "doubt" that their faith would cope if they were to be diagnosed with a terminal disease, or if they faced painful persecution. Such "doubt" may cause them to question the reality of their faith in the present.

Doubt as uncertainty about something you believe to be true

We also use "doubt" to describe the process of questioning things we believe to be true. A scientist who is convinced that evolution is a true theory may begin to "doubt" her belief if new data is discovered that doesn't seem to fit the theory. While she hasn't yet abandoned her belief in evolution—because it still seems the most compelling explanation—she has some new questions that might cause her to rethink.

Or the members of a jury might be utterly convinced that the defendant is guilty after they have heard the prosecution case, but they begin to wonder if the case is so clear cut when they start to hear the defence witnesses. In both cases doubt has been prompted by new information that causes the person to re-evaluate their existing beliefs. In the end they will either reinforce their original belief and hold it more strongly, or have to abandon it.

Doubting in this sense is more akin to questioning our beliefs. It is a process that leads us to change our minds, opinions and convictions. The mere fact that we might have questions about what we believe does not mean that we have ceased to believe. Christians regularly experience doubts like this. They are essential for us to grow and mature. When I was first a Christian, for example, I believed that the children of Christians should be baptised. Over a period of time I began to "doubt" that infant baptism was supported by the Bible, until eventually I became convinced that it wasn't, although I respect the views of Christians who come to a different conclusion. This is just one example where my beliefs and practices have been changed and developed, which began with some element of doubt.

Doubt as lack of assurance

It is important to differentiate such questioning "doubt" from unbelief. Christians may use different language to try to make this distinction. A person may believe that the Christian faith is objectively true, and yet doubt whether they are truly a Christian. Their uncertainty that they are a true believer is a problem of "assurance". The different term helps make clear that this is not the same problem as unbelief. The spiritual remedy for the problem will therefore also be different.

Doubt as unbelief

Finally we sometimes use "doubt" to mean "unbelief". An atheist "doubts" that there is a God. It is ironic that this kind of "doubt" is actually a kind of certainty. Such "doubt" will seem especially incongruous where a person belongs to a group that requires belief in a specific position; for example if a politician belonging to the Scottish Nationalist Party were to campaign against independence because they believe in the maintenance of the United Kingdom. We might use the term "doubt" to describe a church leader who does not believe that Jesus rose from the dead, or of a social church-goer who recites the creed but does not believe what they are saying.

Christians may sometimes be afflicted by limited un-belief. People who profess to be Christians may not believe a particular promise of God, or deny that a specific command of God is true and right. Because the Bible warns against the danger of unbelief it is important to know what beliefs are essential to salvation. It is not essential, for example, to believe that baptism can *only* be by immersion, but *it is essential* to believe that Jesus is fully God.

Doubt is inevitable for Christians

Recognising the broad range of ways in which we use the term "doubt" can be helpful because Christians will inevitably experience "doubt" in at least some of these senses. At times they may question something they believe. This will be good if it leads them to a deeper confidence in the truths of the faith, or to a new conviction which more accurately reflects what God has said in his word. However, we cannot be complacent about our doubts because the Bible warns strongly against the danger of "unbelief."

The heroes of the faith experienced doubt

Many Christians feel a crushing burden of failure and guilt when they experience doubts. This may be compounded because they never hear other Christians admitting to the doubts they experience, and because they hear preachers constantly stressing the importance of faith. They know the stories of great heroes, such as David and Daniel, who trusted God in extraordinary circumstances, and they feel inadequate by comparison.

However, when we read the Bible carefully, we discover that virtually all of God's heroes experienced times of doubt. The greatest chapter on faith is Hebrews 11, which lists the heroes of faith from the Old Testament, and urges us to follow their example. Many of these "heroes" experienced doubt. At times Abraham, the supreme model of faith, doubted that God would keep his promises to him. He twice passed his wife off as his sister because he feared for his life. Even after God had promised him a son, he concocted a plan with his infertile wife to have a child by her slave. His ultimate faith and perseverance were forged through a battle with doubt. The same is true of Moses, Gideon, David, Job and Elijah.

We find the same story in the New Testament. Even when Jesus was with them, the disciples struggled with doubt. Peter doubted that Jesus had to go to Jerusalem to be crucified (Matthew 16 v 22). Thomas famously doubted that Jesus had risen from the dead, but he was not alone. Luke 24 v 38-39 tells us that *all* the disciples found it hard to believe:

> [Jesus] said to them, "Why are you troubled, and why do doubts rise in your minds? Look at my

> hands and my feet. It is I myself! Touch me and
> see; a ghost does not have flesh and bones."

And even after the Holy Spirit had been given at Pentecost, he continued to doubt. Peter doubted when Jesus commanded him to go and preach the gospel to the Gentiles (Acts 10 v 9-23). The New Testament letters repeatedly call their readers to have faith in God. They were written to address their doubts about Jesus and the faith, often prompted by false teachers. James urges believers not to doubt but to pray with faith (James 1 v 6), while Jude commanded the church to be "merciful to those who doubt" (Jude v 22).

The universal Christian experience of struggling with doubt should not surprise us, because we live in a fallen world that has been subjected to darkness and spiritual blindness from the moment that Adam and Eve rebelled in the Garden of Eden. Since then, God's people have been in a spiritual battle for the truth in a world of unbelief. Faith ought to be the real surprise. True faith that triumphs over unbelief is always a miracle of God.

So if you are reading this book because you are struggling with a problem of doubt at the moment, *be encouraged!* The fact that you doubt does not mean that you can't be a Christian. "Doubt" is not the same as "unbelief". Many of the heroes of the Bible, and of church history, have struggled with doubt at some time, as do many of the Christians you know today.

However, you can't afford to ignore your doubt, treating it complacently or just hoping that it will go away. You must deal with it so that it does not develop into unbelief, and use it as an opportunity to develop a more confident, resilient and mature faith.

"None have assurance at all times.
As in a walk that is shaded by trees and chequered
with light and shadow, some tracks and paths are
dark and others are sunshine. Such is usually the life
of the most assured Christian."

Ezekiel Hopkins

Chapter 2

Why is doubt dangerous?

In the previous chapter we saw that doubt is an inevitable experience for the people of God as they live out their faith in a fallen world. While this is a great comfort and reassurance to those who struggle with doubt, it is no reason for complacency. Doubt is dangerous and must be confronted and addressed with urgency by every spiritual resource that is available to Christians and their leaders.

The urgent need to tackle doubt is apparent in the letter to the Hebrews. This letter is an extended pastoral exhortation to Christians who were experiencing doubt and were in danger of abandoning Christianity altogether. They were from a Jewish background, but had heard the gospel and believed that Jesus was the Son of God, who had made atonement for their sins by his death on the cross. They had left the synagogue to join the church, and no longer participated in Jewish sacrifices at the temple.

However, they were experiencing severe doubts that might lead them to give up their faith and return to Judaism. They were questioning whether Jesus was *really* God's promised King, who had fulfilled the promises of the Old Testament; and whether his death had *really* dealt with their sins. Jewish worship was continuing in the temple, and the tangible glory of the high priests and the animal sacrifices that they could see seemed so much more real than what they were experiencing in their new faith. They were also beginning to face increased persecution. Some had been imprisoned and the property of others had been seized.

The unknown author of Hebrews writes into this situation with desperate urgency to persuade them to keep trusting Jesus. He wants them to grasp that Jesus is the full and final revelation from God, the fulfilment of the temple, the true High Priest, and the once-for-all sacrifice for sins. He wants them to appreciate that, despite appearances, what they have in Christ is far more real and glorious than anything the Jews had known.

So, as the Holy Spirit says:
"Today, if you hear his voice,
    do not harden your hearts
as you did in the rebellion,
    during the time of testing in the wilderness,
where your ancestors tested and tried me,
    though for forty years they saw what I did.

That is why I was angry with that generation;
  I said, 'Their hearts are always going astray,
  and they have not known my ways.'
So I declared on oath in my anger,
  'They shall never enter my rest.'"

See to it, brothers and sisters, that none of you has a sinful, unbelieving heart that turns away from the living God. But encourage one another daily, as long as it is called "Today," so that none of you may be hardened by sin's deceitfulness. We have come to share in Christ, if indeed we hold our original conviction firmly to the very end. As has just been said:
"Today, if you hear his voice,
  do not harden your hearts
  as you did in the rebellion."

Who were they who heard and rebelled? Were they not all those Moses led out of Egypt? And with whom was he angry for forty years? Was it not with those who sinned, whose bodies perished in the wilderness? And to whom did God swear that they would never enter his rest if not to those who disobeyed? So we see that they were not able to enter, because of their unbelief.

Therefore, since the promise of entering his rest still stands, let us be careful that none of you be found to have fallen short of it. For we also have had the good news proclaimed to us, just as they did; but the message they heard was of no value

to them, because they did not share the faith of
those who obeyed.   *Hebrews 3 v 7 – 4 v 2*

In this central passage the writer compares his readers'
circumstances with those of the people of Israel in the
wilderness. Even though the Israelites had been freed
from slavery in Egypt, they grumbled about the lack of
food and water, and refused to believe that God would
give them victory over the Canaanites in the promised land. As a result of their unbelief, God condemned
them to die in the desert. This became a warning for
subsequent generations, reflected in Psalm 95, which
is quoted here. The author does not want his readers
to make the same mistake so he urges them to listen to
God and his word.

The questions, challenges and experiences that
cause us to doubt today may not be identical, but the
danger is exactly the same, so the warnings of Hebrews
can be applied to us. The author is passionately concerned for his readers because he is fearful that their
doubts may lead them into unbelief. Nothing less
than their eternal destiny is at stake. If their doubt is
not overcome, they will forfeit their salvation. He fer-
vently hopes that they will come through their period
of doubt with a stronger faith that is more securely
grounded in the truth about Jesus.

Doubt is dangerous because salvation is by faith
The most basic reason why doubt is a danger to Christians is because we receive our salvation solely by faith
in the Lord Jesus. Our greatest problem is that we have

rebelled against God and deserve his just judgment of condemnation to eternal death in hell. There is nothing that we can do to remove this problem of sin for ourselves. There are no rituals that we can perform, or sacrifices that we can offer, that will take away the wrath of God that we deserve. The blood of Jesus is the one and only sacrifice that is able to make effective atonement for our sins.

Jesus came to earth to take the just judgment of God upon himself in our place. He lived a life of perfect obedience to God and then willingly went to the cross. He allowed God to pour out his wrath upon him so that we could be forgiven and saved. Our only hope is to trust what God has done for us through Jesus.

It follows that salvation can only be received as a gift from God through Jesus. Forgiveness, eternal life and a living relationship with God can only be obtained by believing in him. As Jesus famously said:

> For God so loved the world that he gave his
> one and only Son, that whoever believes in him
> shall not perish but have eternal life. For God
> did not send his Son into the world to condemn
> the world, but to save the world through him.
> Whoever believes in him is not condemned, but
> whoever does not believe stands condemned already because they have not believed in the name
> of God's one and only Son.   *John 3 v 16-18*

The New Testament repeatedly confirms that salvation is *only* obtained by faith in Jesus, not by obedience to the requirements of the Jewish law or through doing good works. The stakes of doubt are therefore incredibly high. A person who has put true faith in Jesus has already passed from death to eternal life. Her sins have been forgiven and she has been adopted as a member of God's family. In contrast, a person who has *not* put her faith in Jesus remains unforgiven by God, and she will be condemned to eternal separation from him and his people in hell.

The Bible recognises that some who have professed faith in Jesus will fall away from the "faith". Jesus anticipated this in his Parable of the Sower. The best explanation of the Bible's teaching about this is that those who fall away show that they were never true believers in the first place. However, New Testament authors don't speculate about whether people struggling with doubt are real believers or not. They assume that the faith of professing believers is genuine, and they do everything in their power to encourage them to keep from unbelief.

Doubt is damaging even where it does not lead to unbelief

While the greatest danger is that doubt will turn into full-blown unbelief, it may also have a deeply damaging and disruptive effect on our love and service of the Lord. Unresolved doubt may cause Christians to become unproductive and ineffective. The Bible highlights four specific ways in which doubt may cause damage short of unbelief that disqualifies us from salvation.

1. Doubt may deprive us of the joy of our salvation

True believers are those who have received the gift of salvation by putting their faith in the Lord Jesus and what he has done for them through his death and resurrection. As a result they are saved, and have eternal life, forgiveness of their sins, fellowship with God and a sure and certain hope for the future. These wonderful blessings should bring great joy, a joy that transcends even suffering and persecution.

However, if we lack assurance in our faith, or have doubts about God and his ability to keep his promises to us, then it is unlikely that we will *rejoice* in our salvation. We will be fretful and introspective, turned in on our questions and concerned about our own spiritual wellbeing, rather than looking to God and enjoying his grace. Doubt robs us of the "inexpressible and glorious joy" (1 Peter 1 v 8) that ought to be the experience of those who are "receiving the end result of your faith, the salvation of [your] souls" (v 9).

Doubt will mean that we cannot "consider it pure joy" (James 1 v 2) when we face trials of all kinds. James says that doubt creates something akin to a split personality, causing a person to be "double-minded and unstable in all they do" (v 8). It deprives us of our ability to make decisions and press on with life.

The root cause of a lack of joy in many Christians is unresolved doubt. In some cases this doubt can cause a severe and paralysing spiritual depression, of the kind experienced by the writer of Psalms 42 and 43, who found that his soul was "downcast" and "disturbed".

The loss of joy caused by doubt may be compounded for some believers by the guilt they feel because they are doubting in the first place. This is one reason why it is so important for Christians to face up to their doubts and seek help rather than to repress and deny them.

2. Doubt may deny us answers to our prayers

How and why God answers prayer remains something of a mystery, and the Bible does not explain why he chooses to grant some requests but not others. However, there is evidently a close connection between faith and answered prayer.

This connection is not simplistic and mechanical. The Bible does not teach that our prayers are answered in an automatic way because of the *quantity* of our faith. Paul, for example, prayed three times that the Lord would take away the "thorn in [his] flesh", but Jesus did not do what he asked (2 Corinthians 12 v 7-9). Instead, he supplied Paul with the grace that was sufficient to bear his suffering. It would be wrong to conclude that our prayerful requests are always refused because we lack "faith". Jesus himself taught that our prayers would be powerful and effective if we have faith as small as a mustard seed (Matthew 17 v 20).

While faith does not *guarantee* that our prayers will be answered with a *"yes!"*, doubt will certainly stop us getting what we ask for. James warned his readers that their prayers for wisdom would not be answered if they doubted (James 1 v 5-7).

3. Doubt may distract us from serving Jesus wholeheartedly

Doubt may also keep believers from wholehearted service of God. A believer struggling with doubt may find that their spiritual energy turns inwards because they are consumed by introspection and anxiety.

The distraction that doubt often causes may also result in two apparently opposite responses, both of which reflect the same root problem. **Some who doubt their salvation may throw themselves into serving Jesus as fully as they can to prove to themselves and others that their faith is genuine.** They pour themselves out in evangelism, church ministry and caring for others because they are not sure of their salvation and status in Christ. This hyper-activity is driven by duty and insecurity rather than faith in, and love for, the Lord. Their service will not be marked by joyfulness, but by guilt and fear of never doing enough. While this may look like wholehearted service of Jesus, in reality it is wholehearted service of self. The main motive is to earn the right to feel assured.

Others may respond to doubt by holding back from serving. A person who is unsure of their salvation will find it hard to make sacrifices and take risks for God. Doubt might stop us giving generously to the church and others because we don't trust that God will meet our needs; or from witnessing to Jesus because we fear what others may think of us. Only those with confident faith will follow Jesus even when it means carrying the cross and bearing shame and humiliation in the eyes of the world. Doubt will make us unwilling to pay the full cost of following Christ, because we aren't sure that it will be worth it in the end. We will be unlikely to accept suffering in this world for the sake of Christ unless we are confident in the truth of the resurrection; otherwise we will live like everyone else and "eat and drink, for tomorrow we die" (1 Corinthians 15 v 32).

Elijah is a classic example of a believer whose whole-hearted service of God was curtailed by doubt. In 1 Kings 18 he triumphed over the prophets of Baal in a contest on Mount Carmel. Immediately afterwards, wicked Queen Jezebel sent him a threatening message, promising to take his life by the end of the next day. Rather than trusting God, on the basis of the ample evidence of his power and faithfulness, Elijah fled and refused to continue his ministry. He fell into wallowing in self-pity because his doubt had distorted his perspective on reality. In the New Testament, Timothy was similarly in danger of neglecting the duties of his ministry because he was fearful of suffering for the sake of Jesus, so Paul wrote to him to urge him to be bold and confident in the power of the Holy Spirit .

4. Doubt may disbar us from church ministry and church leadership

Although doubt is a common experience for many Christians, it poses particular problems for those who are involved in Christian ministry and church leadership. It should be obvious that unbelievers have no place as members of the church, let alone in Christian ministry or leadership. All too often, the idea that "doubt" is a mark of honesty, integrity and humility has meant that people have been accepted and appointed as senior church leaders even though they deny core truths of the faith, such as the resurrection or divinity of Jesus. The Bible makes it very clear that a church leader should "hold firmly to the trustworthy message as it has been taught, so that he can encourage others by sound doctrine and refute those who oppose it" (Titus 1 v 9).

While those who deny the core truths of the faith clearly cannot serve in church leadership, those who are experiencing severe and ongoing uncertainty about particular doctrinal truths, the goodness and faithfulness of God, or their own salvation, also ought not to be appointed as leaders. They may still be true believers, but they don't have the spiritual maturity required of leaders. A man who is consistently unsure of the truthfulness of the Bible, for example, ought not to serve as a church leader, home-group leader or Sunday-school teacher until this doubt is resolved.

Leaders who struggle with doubts have a responsibility to ensure that they are resolved, which may require them to take a step back from ministry for a time, and ultimately to resign from their position if their doubts remain. Integrity requires that those who are serving in a church or an organisation that takes a specific position on more secondary matters of the faith, such as baptism, church government, or eschatology, should resign if they can no longer hold to the belief that is required by the body they serve. Their doubt may not disqualify them from ministry altogether, but it does disqualify them from this specific ministry.

How should I respond when friends fall away?

Anyone who has been a Christian for any length of time will have experienced the pain of seeing people who had professed faith stop believing in Jesus. When I was at university, my Christian Union was very encouraged because a first-year student went forward at an evangelistic event and said she had become a Christian. A few weeks later she said she wasn't a Christian after all. Last year I was preaching at a church and met the ex-wife of a man who had seemed to be wonderfully converted. Having been a committed Christian and church member for several years, he tragically announced that he was no longer a believer and was leaving his wife.

The first thing we should do when our friends fall away is to **pray for them and seek to share the gospel with them again, urging them to come back to Christ**. They may be suffering a temporary crisis of faith, but even if they turn away for a long time, we should not give up hope for the possibility of their salvation. They may be as bewildered as everyone else is at their decision to renounce their faith, and value some help in unpicking the reasons why they have changed their thinking. But they still need to trust in Jesus as Lord just as much as anyone else who is not professing faith. We should continue to love them and demonstrate to them the truth of the gospel in our own life (see Jude v 22).

Second, **we should not be surprised or think that God has failed them in some way**. The Bible warns us that people will fall away, and reassures us that this is ultimately their own responsibility and not because

God has let them down. If they never turn back to faith, we can be sure that they were never true believers in the first place.

Third, we should make every effort to **strengthen and protect our own faith**. Satan wants us to worry that perhaps our own faith will fail, but God wants us to do the things that will help us to keep believing: praying, reading his word, gathering with fellow believers for mutual encouragement, and serving him. Perhaps we can learn from those things that contributed to them falling away from the faith. We should use the experience to reflect on what our own faith is based on.

Fourth, if seeing our friends fall away from the faith causes us to realise that we are struggling with doubts of our own, we ought to **seek help from others to make sure that our doubt does not turn into unbelief**. In the same way that seeing a friend diagnosed with cancer might prompt us to take our own symptoms seriously and finally visit a doctor, so the fall of others might prompt us to face up to the seriousness of our situation and seek help.

Doubt may be a chance to grow into more confident faith

While doubt can be dangerous, it also presents an **opportunity to grow into stronger faith and maturity**. Where doubt is addressed and resolved, it may produce deeper joy in salvation, a more confident faith in prayer, and a willingness to live more wholeheartedly and sacrificially for the Lord Jesus. Those who have been tested by doubt and have overcome it are well qualified to serve as leaders in the church.

As we saw at the beginning of the chapter, the author of Hebrews wrote to doubting believers to urge them not to turn away from the faith. He corrected the misunderstandings that had caused them to doubt, and reassured them that persecution was inevitable for those who follow Jesus. He wanted to help them reach a new maturity in the faith:

> We have much to say about this, but it is hard to make it clear to you because you no longer try to understand. In fact, though by this time you ought to be teachers, you need someone to teach you the elementary truths of God's word all over again. You need milk, not solid food! Anyone who lives on milk, being still an infant, is not acquainted with the teaching about righteousness. But solid food is for the mature, who by constant use have trained themselves to distinguish good from evil. Therefore let us move beyond the elementary teachings about Christ and be taken forward to maturity, not laying again the foundation of repentance from acts that lead to death, and of faith in God, instruction about cleansing rites, the laying on of hands, the resurrection of the dead, and eternal judgment. And God permitting, we will do so.   *Hebrews 5 v 11 – 6 v 3*

The same desire to turn doubt into an opportunity for growth and maturity can also be seen in Jesus' ministry. Time and again his disciples displayed ignorance and doubt, but Jesus kept teaching and modelled true faith. In the end they became the bold leaders of the early church.

Doubt is dangerous, but we need not be terrified by it. We must view it as a serious threat, but also as an opportunity for spiritual growth. All the tests and trials that the readers of Hebrews faced were part of the good and wise sovereign plan of God. By facing these challenges, some were exposed as superficial false believers, but others emerged with a stronger faith and greater personal assurance. As Peter wrote to suffering Christians who were facing all kinds of trials:

> These have come so that the proven genuineness of your faith—of greater worth than gold, which perishes even though refined by fire—may result in praise, glory and honour when Jesus Christ is revealed. *1 Peter 1 v 7*

The very circumstances that cause us to doubt may be the means that God uses to test, refine and strengthen our faith.

How do I tell if it's doubt or unbelief?

Imagine someone who is engaged. They have committed to marry their fiancé and are planning their future life on the basis that they expect to share it together. There may be times when they have second thoughts—it's very common. They wonder: "Are we really compatible?" because they learn something new about their fiancé, or they feel attracted to someone else. These second thoughts are like doubts that have to be resisted and worked through, but *the engagement has not been ended.* However, if such doubts become overwhelming, it might lead the person to break off the engagement. At this point the relationship has ended, and the person is no longer planning for a future marriage with their former fiancé.

You are a Christian if you trust and believe that Jesus is the risen Lord, and you are prepared to confess this in public to other people. There may be times when you have second thoughts about whether this is true, but that is not the same as unbelief. You are not an unbeliever until you reject Jesus as Lord. Sadly, Christians sometimes continue to go through the motions of professing faith in Jesus even though they know in their hearts that they have stopped believing. This is like a person who continues with an engagement even though they have decided not to go through with the marriage, because they don't have the courage to break off the engagement.

If you *haven't* rejected Jesus as Lord, and you aren't just pretending to others that you are still a Christian, you are struggling with doubt and not unbelief.

But we also need to be very careful that we are not using our doubts as excuses for escaping the obligation to live for Jesus as Lord. Some years ago I heard senior Christian leader say that when someone tells him: "I'm having doubts about my faith" he asks them: "When did you start sleeping with your girlfriend?" We can use "doubt" as an excuse to justify sinning. When this is the case, it probably means that we have already fallen into unbelief. We would be like a person who is engaged who has not broken off the engagement, but is now dating someone else.

Chapter 3

How can I be sure I am really a Christian?

Many Christians struggle with the fear that they may not be true believers. They don't doubt the truth of the Christian faith, but they lack assurance that they have personally believed and received forgiveness and eternal life. They may lack assurance because they have sinned, are struggling with temptation, or feel that their experience of God is inadequate. Some even assume that it is *arrogant* to have assurance of salvation. They regard doubt as a mark of humility, and an incentive to work hard for God.

By contrast, the New Testament authors write to encourage believers to have confident assurance of their salvation. No letter is more concerned to bring assurance than 1 John. Towards the end of this letter John explains why he has written:

Everyone who believes that Jesus is the Christ is born of God, and everyone who loves the father loves his child as well. This is how we know that we love the children of God: by loving God and carrying out his commands. In fact, this is love for God: to keep his commands. And his commands are not burdensome, for everyone born of God overcomes the world. This is the victory that has overcome the world, even our faith. Who is it that overcomes the world? Only the one who believes that Jesus is the Son of God.

This is the one who came by water and blood—Jesus Christ. He did not come by water only, but by water and blood. And it is the Spirit who testifies, because the Spirit is the truth. For there are three that testify: the Spirit, the water and the blood; and the three are in agreement. We accept human testimony, but God's testimony is greater because it is the testimony of God, which he has given about his Son. Whoever believes in the Son of God accepts this testimony. Whoever does not believe God has made him out to be a liar, because they have not believed the testimony God has given about his Son. And this is the testimony: God has given us eternal life, and this life is in his Son. Whoever has the Son has life; whoever does not have the Son of God does not have life.

I write these things to you who believe in the name of the Son of God so that you may know that you have eternal life.

1 John 5 v 1-13

His letter sets out the basis on which his readers should gain assurance.

What does it mean to be a Christian?

1. A Christian is someone who believes and trusts in Jesus

Many problems of assurance flow from a failure to understand what it means to be a Christian. People wrongly think that being a Christian means being religious, doing good works or having a life-changing spiritual experience. While these might form *part* of the Christian life, they are not the *essence* of what it means to be a Christian. As John makes clear, a Christian is simply someone who has personal faith in Jesus: "Everyone who believes that Jesus is the Christ is born of God" (v 1). So we can't miss his point, he mentions believing in Jesus four other times in the passage.

2. We are saved because of what Jesus has done for us

This emphasis on faith in Jesus makes sense because Christianity is all about what God has done to save us through Jesus. It is not like other world religions, such as Islam or Hinduism, in which salvation depends on doing enough good things to earn God's favour and forgiveness. Such religions can *never* bring assurance of salvation, because it is impossible to know if you have ever done enough. Christianity insists that no human being can ever live a life sufficiently pleasing to God to merit salvation. We all fall short of God's holy standards, and are incapable of obeying God wholeheartedly. We are all sinners who justly deserve to be condemned to hell.

Our "good works" can never be good enough for God so we cannot earn salvation by them. We need a "saviour" who can rescue us from our sin. This is exactly what Jesus came to do. He lived a life of perfect obedience to God, but willingly chose to go to the cross in our place, drinking the cup of God's righteous judgment for us, so that we could be forgiven. He gave his life as a ransom for us, so that we could be forgiven and clothed in his perfect righteousness. We contribute nothing to our salvation.

3. Salvation is God's gift to those who believe and trust in Jesus

Our salvation is *entirely* a gift from God, which we receive by trusting Jesus. John makes this clear in verse 1, where he writes "everyone who believes that Jesus is the Christ is born of God". To be born of God means to have been given the gift of new life and salvation. This metaphor shows that we have not earned or achieved this new life through anything we have done. Rather, "God has given us eternal life, and this life is in his Son" (v 11). Assurance does not depend on what we have done for God, but in trusting in what God has done for us.

What kind of faith is true saving faith?

If the essence of being a Christian is believing in Jesus, then this inevitably raises other questions. *What exactly do you have to believe to be saved?* While urging us to grow to greater understanding and maturity, the New

Testament reassures us that simple faith in Christ is sufficient for our salvation. Jesus said nothing would be impossible for those who have faith as small as a mustard seed (Matthew 17 v 20-21). It is a wonderful encouragement that the simplest faith in Jesus, weak and faltering though it may be, is able to save and bring assurance of eternal life. This is because the saving power of faith is not found in the faith itself, but in the object of faith. It is not *our* faith that saves us, but *Jesus*, so even the smallest faith in him is effective.

1. The content of true saving faith

Even though the smallest faith in Jesus saves, there is an irreducible minimum content to the truth about Jesus that must be understood and believed. John defines true Christians as those who believe that Jesus is "the Christ" and "the Son of God" (1 John 5; John 20 v 30-31). Paul similarly states the minimum content of saving faith in his letter to the Romans:

> If you declare with your mouth, "Jesus is Lord," and believe in your heart that God raised him from the dead, you will be saved. For it is with your heart that you believe and are justified, and it is with your mouth that you profess your faith and are saved.   *Romans 10 v 9-10*

These passages indicate that there can be no salvation unless a person believes these basic truths about Jesus. Those who deny that Jesus was God, perhaps claiming that he was just a great prophet or moral teacher, or deny that he physically rose from the dead, do not have true saving faith. However, we must not demand a greater degree of knowledge and understanding before we encourage people to have assurance. It is not essential to salvation for a person to understand the intricacies of penal substitutionary atonement or justification by faith alone. While we should all strive for greater understanding, which is vital for Christian maturity and the health of the church, it is not the prerequisite for salvation.

2. Believing truths about Jesus is not the same as believing in Jesus

True saving faith is not the same as mere intellectual assent to doctrinal propositions about Jesus. John captures the living and relational nature of true faith by speaking of those who "believe in the name of the Son of God" (1 John 5 v 13). In the culture of the Bible, knowing someone's "name" was a way of indicating that you had a genuine personal relationship with them. James also makes it clear that saving faith requires more than just being able to agree to doctrinal propositions:

> But someone will say, "You have faith; I have deeds." Show me your faith without deeds, and I will show you my faith by my deeds. You believe that there is one God. Good! Even the demons believe that—and shudder.   *James 2 v 18-19*

"Faith" that does not lead to action in our lives, such as

caring for poor fellow Christians, is "dead" (v 17) and cannot save (v 14).

3. Have you trusted Christ?

Given that the basis of assurance is what God has done for us through Jesus, you must start by asking yourself: *"Do I believe and trust in Jesus?"* If the answer is "yes", then you have every entitlement to assurance of salvation. If the answer is "no", then you have no grounds for assurance.

It may be that you can look back to a very specific moment in your life when you put your faith and trust in Jesus, perhaps at church, an evangelistic meeting, on an *Alpha* or *Christianity Explored* course, or at a camp. Remembering how you came to faith might help bring you assurance. But relying on a past experience can lead you to false assurance. *What matters is that you are trusting in Jesus now.*

Alternatively, you *may not* be able to look back to a specific moment when you trusted in Christ. Perhaps you grew up in a Christian family and can never remember a time when you didn't believe in Jesus. Many people don't remember the exact moment they came to faith in Christ. The Bible tells how some people came to a slow dawning realisation that Jesus was the Christ and the Son of God, and it is impossible to know when they first believed. Not everyone has a conversion experience like Paul on the road to Damascus.

The good news is that it doesn't matter that you can't date the precise moment that you came to faith in Christ. That time is known to God. *What matters is that you are trusting in Jesus now*. Present faith is the primary evidence that you have been born again and received God's gift of salvation. So if you believe in your heart that Jesus is the Christ and God's Son, that he died for your sins and rose again, and you are willing to publicly confess that "Jesus is Lord," then you are a Christian and have every right to assurance.

How can I be sure that my faith is genuine?

Even if you *do* believe these things, you may still find that you lack assurance because you doubt that your faith is genuine. You may fear that you are only going through the motions of believing. This is a common problem for those who have a tender conscience and an introverted temperament. The Bible encourages believers afflicted by such doubts. Genuine faith will produce observable and experiential effects in a believer's life. John and the other New Testament writers encourage us to look to both the outward and the inward evidence that proves that our faith is genuine so that we can enjoy assurance.

1. The evidence of a changing life

The first supporting evidence that indicates genuine faith is a changing life. True salvation always results in living a new life. God will be at work in us to change and transform us, producing new attitudes and actions.

John reassures his readers that they have eternal life because he sees evidence that their faith is real. They prove that they have been born of God because they "overcome the world" (1 John 5 v 4). They are resisting the temptations of the culture around them that is fallen and hostile to God. They have not kept sinning in the way they did before they believed (3 v 5-6). Rather than enjoying sin, they increasingly hate it and seek to keep themselves from it. They no longer love and indulge the lusts of their bodies, but want to serve God and please him. They are demonstrating the reality of their faith "by loving God and carrying out his commands" (5 v 2). They have a new love for fellow believers and are willing to share with those in need.

The evidence that convinces John that their faith is genuine is echoed by other New Testament writers. Paul says that Christians will be progressively transformed into the likeness of Jesus and will live a life of love (Romans 8 v 29; 13 v 8-10). The work of the Spirit in their lives will enable them to resist their sinful desires and to develop the fruit of love, joy, peace, forbearance, kindness, goodness, faithfulness, gentleness and self-control (Galatians 5 v 22-23). The author of Hebrews says that true Christians have a growing love for God and his people so they want to meet together for mutual encouragement (Hebrews 10 v 24-25).

In summary, true faith in Jesus will always be evidenced by a new resistance to sin, a new love for God, a new desire to obey his commands and a new love for fellow believers. Those who can see the signs of such changes in their lives have every reason for confident assurance. Peter therefore encourages Christians to "make every effort to confirm their calling and election" by growing in Christian maturity, adding goodness, knowledge, self-control, perseverance, godliness, mutual affection and love to their faith (2 Peter 1 v 10, 5-9).

Sadly, many Christians doubt their faith because they battle against strong and persistent temptations, perhaps sexual temptations especially. But the Bible never promises that we will be fully delivered from sinning, or perfectly conformed to the likeness of Jesus, until our bodies have been resurrected. We are not promised that we will be free of temptation, and we need to remember that temptation is not itself sin (James 1 v 13-15).

The Christian life is a daily battle against the sinful desires of our flesh, which will be in conflict with the new desires that we have to love and serve God, which come from the presence of his Spirit in our hearts (Galatians 5 v 16-18). So don't despair just because you find that you are constantly involved in a battle against temptation to sin. Jesus was tempted. The crucial test is whether you are fighting the battle by hating sin and the idea of sinning, and doing everything you can to resist temptation.

Our assurance may also be undermined when our progress in the Christian life is not *consistent* and *continuous*. There may be times when we stop advancing or we regress. We may stop fighting sin as fiercely. We may find that our love for God and for other Christians has decreased. If we try to assess our faith and progress every day, we will often be discouraged. The New Testament recognises that our progress will vary. Many letters were written to churches that had started well but had backslidden. It is much more helpful to judge our progress and growth over the longer term, and to take periodic stock of how we are doing. At the end of each year, can we see ways in which we have grown in our love for God and for his people? How have we become more Christ-like? Are we resisting sin more determinedly? If we find that our growth has stalled, this should be a wake-up call to repent. The very fact that you are not complacent about spiritual decline or stagnation is a sign of genuine faith. It may be helpful to keep a personal spiritual journal to help assess your progress.

Being objective about yourself

It can be difficult to be objective about your own spiritual progress. Christians often find that their perception of their own progress is masked by a simultaneous growing awareness of their sinfulness. It may be that other people will be more aware of our progress than we are. We need to encourage one another to see the way that the Lord is at work, pointing out the growth that we see in each other. Almost all the New Testament authors share encouragements in their letters of what they see in the faith of their readers—such as their progress in godliness, love and service—even when they are pointing out other failings.

True believers may commit terrible sins that inevitably call into question the reality of their salvation. However, if this leads to genuine repentance and true sorrow, then it indicates that there is a genuine faith. As John writes in his letter:

> If we claim to be without sin, we deceive ourselves and the truth is not in us. If we confess our sins, he is faithful and just and will forgive us our

sins and purify us from all unrighteousness. If we claim we have not sinned, we make him out to be a liar and his word is not in us. My dear children, I write this to you so that you will not sin. But if anybody does sin, we have an advocate with the Father—Jesus Christ, the Righteous One. He is the atoning sacrifice for our sins, and not only for ours but also for the sins of the whole world.

1 John 1 v 8 – 2 v 2

There is no sin that is too bad, or too often repeated, to be forgiven through the death of Christ. His death can save from all the sins committed in history, both those committed before and after he came to earth. The Bible records the serious sins and failures of many believers—such as Peter's denial of Christ, David's adultery with Bathsheba and a member of the Corinthian church who was sleeping with his father's wife—so that we can be sure that our sins as believers will be forgiven if we repent and seek God's mercy as they did.

If you are struggling with assurance because you have sinned in some *specific* way, perhaps secretly so that no one else knows what you have done, you need to confess your sin to God and trust his promise of forgiveness and cleansing. Jesus has already paid the price for what you have done. Your repentance might require you to confess to other believers, perhaps your pastor or church elders, and bear the shame of your action.

You may need to seek forgiveness from those you have sinned against, and make restitution to those you have harmed. However, your heartfelt repentance is good evidence of the genuineness of your faith and ought to bring great assurance. You may feel that you *cannot* be forgiven—but there is no sin too bad to be forgiven by God, except the unforgivable sin of rejecting Jesus.

2. The evidence of God's presence with us by his Holy Spirit

True faith produces changes in our experiences, not just in our actions, because it brings about a new relationship with God. The Bible tells us that we will experience the work and presence of the Holy Spirit in our lives, confirming the reality of this relationship and bringing assurance of our salvation. John refers to this subjective experience in his letter, where he writes that God has provided testimony to the truth that Jesus is the Son of God through his Spirit, and that those who have believed in Jesus have come to accept this testimony (1 John 5 v 6-10). Earlier in his letter he is even more explicit about the assuring presence of the Spirit in believers:

> This is how we know that we live in him and he in us: he has given us of his Spirit. And we have seen and testify that the Father has sent his Son to be the Saviour of the world. If anyone acknowledges that Jesus is the Son of God, God lives in them and they in God. And so we know and rely on the love God has for us.   *1 John 4 v 13-16*

While John does not explain what this experience feels like, Paul helps us to understand what to expect as a result of the indwelling presence of the Holy Spirit. In Romans 8 v 14-17 he writes:

> For those who are led by the Spirit of God are the children of God. The Spirit you received does not make you slaves, so that you live in fear again; rather, the Spirit you received brought about your adoption to sonship. And by him we cry, "*Abba*, Father." The Spirit himself testifies with our spirit that we are God's children. Now if we are children, then we are heirs—heirs of God and co-heirs with Christ, if indeed we share in his sufferings in order that we may also share in his glory.

Paul is saying that true believers will be given some subjective experiential personal awareness that they are children of God. He does not say that we will feel this *all the time*, nor that it is an *intense or overwhelming experience of joy* and awareness of the Lord's presence. The context suggests that this assurance is given in tough circumstances when we face suffering and opposition, and that it will be accompanied by groaning and frustration at having to continue to live in a fallen world.

Many Christians lack assurance because they have unrealistic expectations of what the Christian life should *feel* like, perhaps because they compare their own experience with what they hear others say about their walk with the Lord, or what they have read of the lives of great believers of the past. It is essential to distinguish carefully between what God can do for his people, and what he promises to do for them. The New

Testament shows that Christians may experience the work of the Spirit in their lives in many ways, but this does not mean that these experiences are promised to *all* believers. Flawed Biblical interpretation, theological naiveté and spiritual enthusiasm easily treat exceptional experiences as if they were "the normal Christian life". They are not!

I don't have "big experiences" of God—so how can I be sure?

We read in the Bible about people who have tremendous experiences of God's presence and power. And when we hear other people talking about their amazing experiences or read an exciting Christian biography, it can be easy to feel that everyone else is having an experience of God that is completely missing from our own lives.

It's common to hear people say is that God wants to give all believers an overwhelming experience of the love and presence of the Holy Spirit, which will bring them so much assurance that they are God's child that they will never doubt again. This experience has been termed "sealing with the Spirit." This is a misuse of biblical language, and creates a false expectation. Christians are "sealed" with the Holy Spirit when they are converted, as a mark of the fact that they belong to God and as a guarantee of their inheritance (see Ephesians 1 v 13-14; 2 Corinthians 1 v 22). God may be pleased to make his presence and love known to us in a remarkable and overwhelming way, and many believers can testify to such experiences from time to time, but God does not promise to grant such experiences to every believer.

We should not, therefore, expect the inner witness of the Holy Spirit to the fact that we are true children of God to be a single, overwhelming experience. We should not doubt our salvation just because we have not had the same experiences as others. God does not promise equality of spiritual experiences to his people. We are all different, and our individual relationship with God is unique.

However, if we are true believers in the Lord Jesus, we *should* expect that from time to time we will experience an inner confidence that we have been adopted as God's child and have entered into a living relationship with him. This inner confidence leads us to cry out to him as our Father. We must not ignore such simple and apparently unremarkable experiences of God's loving assurance by his Spirit. There are other signs: every time we are disgusted by sin, every time we are grateful to Jesus for what he has done for us, every time we hunger to be more holy, every time we choose to follow his ways rather than our own—these are experiences of the work of the Spirit in our lives, and signs that we truly belong to him. They are the evidence that we are true believers. Remembering them is an important spiritual discipline. Again, it can be helpful to keep a spiritual journal of those times when we have known and experienced the witness of the Spirit in our lives.

Another common error that undermines assurance is the teaching that the Spirit is only given to believers as a second experience after conversion, accompanied by speaking in tongues. This is wrongly termed "baptism in the Spirit". There is no solid biblical support for this idea. The New Testament says that Christians receive the Spirit when they believe (eg: 1 Corinthians 12 v 13), and only *some* Christians are given the gift of tongues (1 Corinthians 12 v 30; 14 v 5). While believers may enjoy experiences of the presence and power of the Holy Spirit subsequent to their conversion, which the New Testament calls being "filled" with the Spirit, and such experiences may bring great assurance, neither an experience of "Baptism in the Spirit" nor speaking in tongues should be the basis of our assurance.

Summary

God wants us to have confident assurance of our salvation. Far from making us arrogant and lazy, this enables us to endure suffering and opposition as we wait patiently for Jesus to return, and motivates us to serve him joyfully and wholeheartedly.

Sadly, many Christians lack the assurance that they could enjoy because they misunderstand the basis of assurance, or because they have mistaken expectations of what a genuine Christian life will feel like. John wrote his letter so that his readers would know that they had eternal life. He invited them to examine themselves and see the evidence that their faith was genuine. Paul similarly invited the Corinthians to examine themselves "to see whether you are in the faith" (2 Corinthians 13 v 5). We should examine ourselves, and encourage each other to see the grace of God at work in our lives, so that we can enjoy the assurance God intends for us.

So ask yourself these questions:

- Do I believe and trust today that Jesus is the Christ and the Son of God, who died for my sins and rose from the dead?

- Has my life changed since I put my faith and trust in Jesus? Can I honestly say that I have developed a greater love for God, a love for his word, a love for his people and a hatred of sin? Do I struggle to resist temptation, and when I sin am I quick to repent with genuine sorrow for what I have done? Have others been able to see ways in which I have changed, and have they observed me make progress in godliness and Christ-like character over time?

- Have I experienced something of the work and witness of the Holy Spirit in my life, causing me to cry out to God as my Father and confirming to me that I am his child?

How can I be sure that God loves me?

It's very common for people who believe wholeheartedly that the Christian faith is true to struggle in believing that God truly loves them personally. This may be because they are deeply conscious of their own sinfulness and failure, so that they feel unlovable to a holy God, or because they don't have any feelings of God's love towards them, or because they are experiencing difficulties and suffering in their life which make them question whether God really cares for them.

Part of the problem is that our relationship with God is not identical to our other human relationships. We cannot see God face to face. Instead, he makes himself known to us through his word, supremely through his Son, the Lord Jesus. So our relationship with God is *mediated* rather than *direct* and sensory, and this side of death it is not the same as our relationship with, for example, our human parents, our spouse or our friends.

We are called to live by faith rather than by sight, and our assurance of God's love comes ultimately from what he has done for us in history. God has proved his love for us through Jesus. In Romans 5 v 8 Paul writes to encourage suffering Christians to be sure that God loves them, and tells them that the cross is like God's giant Valentine's card, declaring his love to them:

"God demonstrates his own love for us in this: while we were still sinners, Christ died for us."

This truth is tremendously reassuring. It reminds us that God's love for us is not based on anything that makes us lovable to him. He does not love us because we love him (see also 1 John 4 v 10). He does not love us because we are good, or at least not too bad. He chose to love us while we were still his enemies and hostile to him. He sent his precious Son to die one of the most painful and horrible deaths imaginable on our behalf because we were sinners who deserved his judgment.

And he still loves us even though we continue to sin, because he has already declared us to be righteous in his sight because of our faith in Jesus. The sufferings and hardships we face are not an indication that he has stopped loving us, but rather, are proof that he is working out his loving purpose to transform us into the likeness of Jesus (see Romans 8 v 28-30, 37), and that he is training us as a loving father would his children (Hebrews 12 v 7-11).

The Bible does not promise that we will *feel* the love of God directly as an emotional experience. We will certainly experience the consequences of his love for us as we enjoy peace, forgiveness and joy, and as we are moved to love him, obey his commands, and love others (Romans 5 v 5; 1 John 4 v 7-21). However, we should not look to our subjective emotional experiences as the basis for knowing that God loves us. The times when we will most need to be sure of the love of God are when we sin or suffer, and these are the times when our experience is least likely to bring us assurance of God's love.

Instead, we need to look to the cross and what God has already done for us there. The fact that he sent Jesus to the cross proves once for all eternity that he loves us. As John writes in his letter:

> This is how God showed his love among us: he sent his one and only Son into the world that we might live through him. This is love: not that we loved God, but that he loved us and sent his Son as an atoning sacrifice for our sins.
>
> *1 John 4 v 9-10*

"Feelings of confidence about our salvation need to be tested before they are trusted."

J I Packer

Chapter 4

How can I overcome doubt as a Christian?

Ten years ago Dan Brown published his best-selling thriller, *The Da Vinci Code*. This claimed to be based on fact and alleged that the Christian faith was a huge conspiracy perpetrated by the Emperor Constantine and the Catholic Church. Jesus was not God but just a man, who had married Mary Magdalene and had children. The accurate accounts of the life of Jesus had been suppressed and excluded from the Bible.

Because this book included many accurate historical details, it caused some Christians to doubt their faith. Could they really trust the Bible as a true record of the life, claims and teachings of Jesus? Had the church perpetrated a huge fraud? In response to the run-away success of the book a number of reputable scholars, both Christians and non-Christians, set out to debunk its claims. Those who found their faith threatened were helped to overcome their doubts. In many cases their faith was strengthened because they were now better informed about the truthfulness of the Bible and how the earliest Christians had worshipped Jesus as God from the beginning.

The story of *The Da Vinci Code* helps us to understand one way that doubt can be caused, and what we need to do to counter it. As we have seen in previous chapters, many Christians will battle against doubt, but we can have confidence that this battle can be won. Many New Testament letters were written to counter doubts troubling Christians. A classic example of a passage tackling a problem of doubt is 2 Peter 3 v 3-10:

> Above all, you must understand that in the last days scoffers will come, scoffing and following their own evil desires. They will say, "Where is this 'coming' he promised? Ever since our ancestors died, everything goes on as it has since the beginning of creation." But they deliberately forget that long ago by God's word the heavens came into being and the earth was formed out of water and by water. By these waters also the world of that time was deluged and destroyed. By the same word the present heavens and earth are reserved for fire, being kept for the day of judgment and destruction of the ungodly.
>
> But do not forget this one thing, dear friends: with the Lord a day is like a thousand years, and a thousand years are like a day. The Lord is not slow in keeping his promise, as some understand

slowness. Instead he is patient with you, not wanting anyone to perish, but everyone to come to repentance.

But the day of the Lord will come like a thief. The heavens will disappear with a roar; the elements will be destroyed by fire, and the earth and everything done in it will be laid bare.

2 Peter was written to help Christians exposed to false teaching. Here Peter tackles their doubts that Jesus will return. In response to mocking sceptics, he reassures his readers that Jesus will keep his promise. He reminds us that God has kept promises of judgment in the past, and explains that God's view of time is not the same as ours. What seems like a long delay to us is nothing from his perspective.

In this chapter we will consider what we can do to overcome our doubts and develop a more confident faith.

Admit that you are struggling with doubt and seek help

The first and most important step to overcoming doubt is to face up to the fact that you are struggling in your faith. Many Christians are too embarrassed to admit that they have doubts. And sadly, some churches are condemning and critical of those who experience doubt, which can make it difficult for people to seek help from others.

But as we have seen, doubt is a normal experience for Christians, and we should not have to suffer in silence. It is best nipped in the bud, rather than being allowed to grow and fester to the point where it might turn into unbelief or apostasy.

We will never be able to address our doubts if we are in denial and pretend we don't have a problem. The author of Psalm 42 had to admit that his soul was downcast before he was able to minister to himself and renew his hope in God. If you are struggling with issues of doubt, you need to seek the help of Jesus and of mature believers who know the Bible and love God, who will be able to listen to you, pray with you and speak the truth of the gospel into your life.

Come to Jesus for help with your doubt

Christians who are struggling with doubt often feel that the last thing they can do is come to God for help. They suspect God will be angry with them because they doubt, and so they foolishly try to hide their doubts from him, as if he does not know the state of their hearts already. They do not turn to him in prayer, assuming that he will not want to listen to them.

However, the *very first thing* that we should do when we are troubled by doubt is to come to God through Jesus, and tell our loving heavenly Father how we are struggling, and ask that he would be merciful and help us to overcome our doubts. We can come to Christ with confidence that he will be sympathetic and understand our struggles, because he was tempted to doubt during his earthly life. When he was tested in the wilderness, Satan tempted him to doubt his identity as the Son of God, to doubt that God would protect him from harm, and to doubt that he had to go to the cross to gain his kingdom (Matthew 4 v 1-11). Jesus resisted these temptations and did not succumb to unbelief, but his experience means that he knows what it is like to be tempted to doubt. The author of the letter to the Hebrews urged his readers, who we have seen were being tempted into unbelief, to turn to Jesus and seek his help:

> For we do not have a high priest who is unable to feel sympathy for our weaknesses, but we have one who has been tempted in every way, just as we are—yet he did not sin.   *Hebrews 4 v 15*

So if you are struggling with doubt, cry out to Jesus for help. He will understand. Tell him why you are doubting, and ask him to help you overcome your doubts. Cry to him just like the father in Mark 9 v 24: *"I do believe; help me overcome my unbelief"*. You can be confident that your relationship with God does not depend on your faith being perfect. Your relationship with God is secure because you have been united with Christ and justified in the sight of God. You have been clothed in his perfect righteousness, which he obtained by living a life of complete obedience and faith. He never fell into the sin of unbelief so all your doubts are covered by his perfect faith, which is counted as yours.

Seek the help of mature believers with your doubt

When we are struggling with doubt we should also seek the help of fellow believers. We have not just been saved as isolated individuals but Jesus has made us members of his family, the church, and we have been given many brothers and sisters to help us in our journey of faith. Job was right to seek help from his friends when he was struggling with doubt, even though they proved inadequate to the task. If you are struggling with doubt you should try to find a mature Christian friend you can talk with, who will commit to pray *for* you and *with* you. You should also seek the help of your church leaders. You may feel afraid to speak to them about your doubts, but they will be delighted that you want their help.

However, you shouldn't speak to *everyone* about your doubt. Sharing your doubts with others can be damaging to them, and can undermine their confidence in the faith. The author of Psalm 73 testified how he had come through a time of doubting about whether God was truly good. When he was wrestling with this doubt, he chose not to speak about his struggles to the people of God as a whole, so that he would not lead others astray:

> If I had spoken out like that, I would have be-
> trayed your children.   *Psalm 73 v 15*

It is better to speak in confidence to those who are best placed to help you.

If someone comes to you for help with their doubts, make sure you don't react judgmentally. Rather "be merciful to those who doubt" (Jude v 22). Listen carefully to what they have to say and don't offer simplistic platitudes. Pray for them and with them, and make sure that you point them to the Bible for answers and to the Lord Jesus as the object of their faith. Don't gossip with others about their struggles, but encourage them to speak with their church leader. Offer to go with them so that they do not feel alone and embarrassed. In many cases you may not be able to help a person with doubts because you don't know enough to answer their questions. Where this is the case, the most important thing you can do is to ensure that they are able to speak to someone who will be able to help.

Identify the root causes of your doubt

A doctor can only treat a patient effectively if he first rightly diagnoses the disease and its cause. In the same way doubts can only be addressed if their root causes are identified. The authors of the New Testament demonstrate great pastoral skill in identifying the causes of their readers' doubts, and then applying the truth of the gospel to strengthen their faith.

There are a number of common causes of doubt, several of which may be operative at the same time. It can be helpful to think of doubts that are primarily rooted in our bodies, minds, hearts and spirits.

1. Doubt rooted in our bodies: Physical causes of doubt

Sometimes our doubts are the result of physical rather than spiritual problems. Human beings are a complex whole, so our physical wellbeing impacts on our thoughts, feelings and spiritual life. Periods of doubt may be the result of tiredness, exhaustion, illness, depression, or the onset of tragic conditions like dementia. Jesus experienced intense periods of testing when he was hungry or exhausted.

Where doubt is the result of physical causes, we need to address the underlying physical or medical issue, not spiritualise it. Simply getting a good night's sleep, eating a good meal, taking exercise, having a day off or a holiday, or allowing PMT to pass may be sufficient to relieve doubt. In the case of longer term physical or medical problems, such as depression or mental illness, appropriate treatment will be needed.

2. Doubt rooted in our minds:
Intellectual causes of doubt

We were created by God with minds designed for rational thought. Even though our minds are renewed when we come to faith in Christ (Romans 12 v 2), we remain susceptible to intellectual arguments that seem to call into question the truth of our faith.

Christians confronted with a new idea, new information, new evidence or a new argument may find their faith is unsettled, especially when these ideas are put forward by a purported "expert". A Christian who has taken it for granted that world was made in six literal days just 6000 years ago may find their faith challenged if they are confronted by some scientific evidence they have never had to consider before. A new Christian may find her faith disturbed and threatened when she reads in the Bible that God commanded the Israelites to kill all the inhabitants of Canaan, because she cannot see how a loving God could do this.

The Bible is packed with examples where the authors

address such intellectual doubts. We have already seen how Peter assured his readers that Jesus would return. Earlier in his letter he countered the claim that he had simply made up his stories about Jesus:

> For we did not follow cleverly devised stories when we told you about the coming of our Lord Jesus Christ in power, but we were eye-witnesses of his majesty. He received honour and glory from God the Father when the voice came to him from the Majestic Glory, saying, "This is my Son, whom I love; with him I am well pleased." We ourselves heard this voice that came from heaven when we were with him on the sacred mountain.
>
> *2 Peter 1 v 16-18*

Paul devoted a whole chapter of 1 Corinthians to demolishing the arguments of those who thought that the idea of a physical, bodily resurrection was ridiculous and unbelievable.

Intellectual doubts need to be countered by better arguments and better evidence. This is what the Christian church has done for the last two thousand years. It should be a tremendous reassurance that there are no completely new challenges to the Christian faith. Most of the major objections have been thoroughly investigated and answered by outstanding thinkers down the centuries. Christians who are struggling with intellectual questions can find help from those who are able to answer their questions, or who can point them to useful books and resources. Or there's a list of suggestions on page 95.

At the same time there are some questions that we can *never* answer adequately or conclusively. We can only know with certainty what God has revealed to us in the Bible, and there are many things that God has chosen not to reveal or explain. As Deuteronomy 29 v 29 puts it: "the secret things belong to the LORD". God does not, for example, explain how it was possible for Jesus to be both fully man and God, nor how he can be three persons but one God in the Holy Trinity. God does not explain why specific individuals suffer, or why some people suffer so much more than others.

Sometimes we have to be honest enough to admit that we don't have a complete answer to an intellectual objection to the faith. However, our confidence in what we do know for certain about God enables us to trust him anyway. In every field of human knowledge, including science, there are many things that we don't know and can't ever know, but we are prepared to trust on the basis of what we do know with certainty.

3. Doubts rooted in our hearts:
Experiential and emotional causes of doubt

While doubt may involve a significant intellectual element, it is rarely just an intellectual problem. For some Christians their natural temperament makes them prone to doubt, and they may struggle with worry and anxiety in other areas of their life. Others doubt because their experience of life in the world does not match up with what they believe about God.

The apparent inconsistency between what we believe ought to be the case, and what we actually experience, causes us to doubt the faith. This is commonly the case when we experience suffering, or watch others endure suffering. Job, for example, was not caused to doubt by intellectual questions about how God could allow suffering in the world. Job knew full well that there was great suffering in the world, and he had worked for justice and cared for widows and the poor. He doubted because he and his family were directly afflicted by *suffering*. Many of the psalms express the struggle for faith of people wrestling with suffering, who are in anguish because God does not seem to have blessed them and kept his promises to his people.

Our exposure to other people and life experiences may also prompt us to question the truth of our faith. A Christian who falls in love with a girl at work who wants to start a sexual relationship may begin to doubt that God says that sex is only for marriage. A Christian who befriends a deeply spiritual Hindu who works tirelessly for the good of the community may begin to question whether Jesus really is the only way to God.

There are no easy answers to the doubts that are rooted in our experiences and emotions. In the end all doubt is a battle between trusting the word of God and trusting our own feelings and intuitions about reality.

When we are faced with the *fact* of suffering, do we believe that God is sovereign and working out his good purpose, even though we may not be able to see and understand what that may be? Or do we conclude that there is no God, or at least that there is no just, fair and loving God?

In the Bible we see believers allowing the truth of God's word to interpret their experiences, rather than allowing their experiences to determine what they believe about God. In Psalm 73 the Psalmist doubted the goodness of God to his people when he compared their struggles with the apparent health and prosperity of the wicked. His doubt was not resolved until he allowed God to change his perspective:

> When I tried to understand all this,
> > it troubled me deeply
> till I entered the sanctuary of God;
> > then I understood their final destiny
> > > *Psalm 73 v 16-17*

His own circumstances were not changed; nor did the wicked suddenly stop enjoying a comfortable life. However, he understood that the present state of affairs was not the end of the story. He was enabled to interpret his experience in the light of the revelation of God.

In a similar way Job was only able to overcome his doubts about God's justice and fairness when he experienced his presence and heard his word. God did not answer Job's questions, or explain why he and his family had suffered. Job stopped asking and was rendered silent in repentance and renewed faith.

Paul also wrote to reassure Christians in Rome that their sufferings did not invalidate the truth of the gospel. They needed to have confidence in God's good purposes for them, and to trust in his ultimate victory:

> And we know that in all things God works for
> the good of those who love him, who have been
> called according to his purpose ... For I am con-
> vinced that neither death nor life, neither angels
> nor demons, neither the present nor the future,
> nor any powers, neither height nor depth, nor
> anything else in all creation, will be able to sepa-
> rate us from the love of God that is in Christ Jesus
> our Lord.   *Romans 8 v 28, 38*

In the end doubt can only be overcome by trusting God's word and his promises rather than believing the voices of others or drawing our own conclusions about reality from our experiences and our emotions. We need to have our thinking corrected by God's word, and then to bring our feelings and emotions into line with that truth.

Our culture draws a sharp distinction between our thinking and our emotions, between "head" and "heart". The Bible's understanding is very different. The heart is an integrated whole, comprising our thinking, will and emotions. It is the decision-making centre of our personality, and is not just subject to the vagaries of our feelings. The task of the heart is to orientate our life, deciding what direction we will take. The only way to overcome our doubts is to allow God's word to de-termine the decisions of our heart, transforming our thinking and changing our emotions so that we allow him to interpret our experiences, rather than allowing our experiences to determine our thinking about him.

This is a long and continual process that requires

being re-acquainted with the majesty and character of God and listening attentively to his word. Our doubts may not be resolved quickly or easily, but this is the only way that we will be able to resolve them, or perhaps to cling onto our faith, trusting that God knows the answers even if we are unable to finally resolve the doubts ourselves.

4. Doubt rooted in our spirits: Spiritual causes of doubt

While it is helpful to identify physical, intellectual and experiential causes of doubt, we must never forget that we are also involved in a spiritual battle. Christians have an implacably hostile enemy whose objective is to destroy our faith or render it ineffective. From the very beginning in the Garden of Eden, Satan's tactic has been to persuade God's people to doubt his word and rebel against him. Our struggles with doubt are part of our wider spiritual struggle against Satan.

Satan does his work through many human agents and agencies. He is a liar, and his lies are disseminated by those who deny the truth of God and his word. His lies dominate the world in which we live. We are in hostile territory and the messages proclaimed by the culture around us—in the media, entertainment or education— undermine God's word and seek to stimulate doubt and unbelief. Satan stirs up persecution against God's people by authorities, government and individuals, in the hope that such persecution will cause our faith to buckle.

While we must always be on guard against this general satanic deception, there are times when Satan may target individual believers more directly. Jesus was subjected to the most intense personal temptation in the desert when Satan sought to persuade him to doubt God. Job's suffering was also instigated by Satan to test his faith. The psalmists and prophets relate experiences of great spiritual darkness and despair, and some Christians testify to times when they have experienced the apparent absence of God and abandonment by him.

We are commanded to stand firm against the devil and his strategies. We must put on the "full armour of God" (Ephesians 6 v 10-17), which is the truth of the gospel and the blessings we enjoy through it, so that we are protected from the enemy. If we submit ourselves to God and resist the devil, we can be sure that "he will flee" (James 4 v 7). Even though he is fierce and dangerous, Satan is a defeated enemy because of the victory of Jesus on the cross. He has no power over Christians. As the book of Job reveals, Satan is subject to the sovereignty of God and can only act in ways that God allows.

Addressing the causes of doubt

Whatever the primary causes of your doubt, the only answer is to come back to the truth of the word of God. Doubt is a battle for the truth. Will we believe the truth of God's word about himself or the claims of those who deny it? Will we believe our intuitions and emotions or what God says? Will we believe God or Satan?

In the end, the Christian faith stands or falls on whether Jesus really was the divine Son of God, who took on human flesh, was crucified and rose again after three days. If this really happened, then we can be sure that God exists. We can know what God is like because Jesus fully reveals him to us. We can be sure that the Bible, both Old and New Testament, is true because Jesus tells us so. We can be confident that God is love, and that he will accomplish his good purposes for his people. We can trust that our sufferings are part of his good plan for us, even though we may not understand how, because we can see that Jesus entered into glorious new life after the suffering of the cross. We can trust that Jesus will return to bring true justice and remake our broken world.

If we can be confident about Jesus, then this is the basis from which we can address all our doubts. This does not mean that we have the answer to every question that troubles us. Rather, we will be able to trust that those questions are answered in Jesus. Our trust in him will be so sure that it can transcend the arguments, experiences, emotions or spiritual attacks that cause us to doubt. The cross demonstrates for us, once and for all, the vastness of God's love, and shows how even the wicked intentions of men and Satan are turned to accomplish God's good purpose.

Faith does not require that all our questions are answered, nor that everything makes sense to us now. It trusts in what has been clearly revealed by God, supremely in Jesus himself. It is content to leave the uncertainties with him. Confidence in what has been revealed is able to trump doubts and uncertainties.

This is why the claims made in *The Da Vinci Code* were so potentially destructive to Christian faith. If Jesus was not the divine Son of God, who makes God known to us in the fullest way that we can access in this world, then we are left with nothing but speculation or wishful thinking. This cannot overcome the doubts that trouble us. However, if Jesus really is the divine Son of God, his revelation to us gives us a firm basis for our faith, from which we can resist our doubts.

The final answer to doubt is to turn back to Jesus and to consider the evidence for him, so that we believe his word and base our lives on his promises. Luke and John both wrote their Gospels, based on eyewitness testimony, so that we can do this (Luke 1 v 1-4; John 20 v 30-31). Confident faith in Jesus is something we have to nurture all the time—and we will think about how we can do that in the next chapter.

What is the gift of faith mentioned in the Bible?

Paul mentions the gift of faith in his list of spiritual gifts in 1 Corinthians 12 v 9. But what exactly is this gift?

It's important that we interpret this phrase in its specific context, and that we do not assume that Paul uses the word "faith" in the same way everywhere in his letters. Here Paul is listing a series of special gifts or abilities that are given to Christians by the Holy Spirit to enable them to do the work of ministry that will build up the church. This gift of faith is listed alongside the message of wisdom, message of knowledge, healing, miraculous powers, prophecy, distinguishing between spirits, speaking in different kinds of tongues and the interpretation of tongues.

Paul's whole point is that God gives these gifts to Christians as he determines in his sovereignty—but we do not all have the same gifts. Not every Christian will have the gift of "tongues", and therefore not every Christian will have the gift of "faith" (see v 4-6 and 27-30). Given the context, Paul *cannot* be speaking about the simple belief and trust in Jesus that brings salvation, because every true Christian has this saving faith.

It is difficult to know today precisely what Paul means by some of the spiritual gifts; so for example Christians debate whether the gift of tongues is the miraculous ability to speak in other human languages or a spiritual language. Most likely the gift of faith here is a special measure of faith that a person is given in a specific situation that God can act in supernatural power. It is described in 13 v 2 as "a faith that can move mountains." This gift was perhaps evident when Jesus saw that the four men who had brought their paralysed friend to him had "faith" (Luke 5 v 20), or when Paul was preaching in Lystra and knew that a man who was lame from birth "had faith to be healed" (Acts 14 v 9).

"Doubt indulged soon becomes doubt realised."

Frances Ridley Havergal

Chapter 5

How can I develop a confident faith?

In the last two chapters we have seen how Christians can overcome a lack of assurance and specific doubts about their faith. While there will be times when we have to confront specific doubts, we should also take proactive measures to nurture and strengthen our faith so that we are not as susceptible to doubt.

One great danger for western Christians is our individualism. The philosopher René Descartes famously withdrew into isolation so that he could doubt *everything* in his futile attempt to find a firm foundation for true knowledge outside of God. God's people are not meant to live lonely, isolated lives, which is a recipe for doubt. God saves us *into* his new community, the church, and we are called to face the challenges of faith together with our brothers and sisters. Jesus also faced his greatest times of testing when he was alone.

The New Testament letters model how the church

should work as a family—supporting and encouraging one another in the truth of the gospel. For example, Paul wrote to Christians in Thessalonica who had become disturbed about the fate of believers who died before Jesus returned:

> Brothers and sisters, we do not want you to be uninformed about those who sleep in death, so that you do not grieve like the rest of mankind, who have no hope. For we believe that Jesus died and rose again, and so we believe that God will bring with Jesus those who have fallen asleep in him. According to the Lord's word, we tell you that we who are still alive, who are left until the coming of the Lord, will certainly not precede those who have fallen asleep. For the Lord himself will come down from heaven, with a loud command, with the voice of the archangel and with the trumpet call of God, and the dead in Christ will rise first. After that, we who are still alive and are left will be caught up together with them in the clouds to meet the Lord in the air. And so we will be with the Lord for ever. Therefore encourage one another with these words.
>
> *1 Thessalonians 4 v 13-18*

He corrects the misunderstandings that are causing them to doubt, and explains that those who have already died will not miss out when Jesus returned. He commands them to "encourage one another with these words". He wants them to become a community that is speaking the truth of God's word to each other about the hope of those who have died in faith. He wants them to remind each other that, whether they are alive when Jesus returns or have died beforehand, their glorious destiny is to "be with the Lord for ever". If they do this, they will be protected against doubt, just as a vaccination protects against infection.

Here we will consider some of the vital "spiritual disciplines" we need to practise if we are to resist doubt and develop a strong, mature and resilient faith.

Maintain a close personal walk with God

The Christian life is often pictured as a "walk". Disciples are called to follow the Lord Jesus, listening to his voice and learning from his example. As we make this journey, we will face many temptations to go in a different direction and follow other voices. We therefore need to ensure that we maintain a "close walk" with Jesus, keeping in step with him and his Spirit.

Jesus uses the metaphor of a sheep and a shepherd to describe his relationship with his disciples. His disciples must listen to his voice and follow him:

> The one who enters by the gate is the shepherd of the sheep. The gatekeeper opens the gate for him, and the sheep listen to his voice. He calls his own sheep by name and leads them out. When he has brought out all his own, he goes on ahead of them, and his sheep follow him because they know his voice. But they will never follow a stranger; in

fact, they will run away from him because they do not recognise a stranger's voice. *John 10 v 2-5*

We cultivate a close personal walk with Jesus by careful and attentive listening to the word of Christ, and depending on him for all our needs in prayer. Hearing God's word preached and praying together are core elements of the corporate life of the church—and regularly sitting under God's word is vital for our spiritual health and growth. But we also need to cultivate personal communion with God. We need to read the Bible regularly, prayerfully and carefully.

Psalm 1 declares that the man who is blessed and fruitful has his "delight ... in the law of the LORD" and he "meditates on [it] day and night" (Psalm 1 v 2). And we have the full revelation of Jesus in the New Testament, the principle is the same. We need to listen to the word of God and make it the basis of our lives. When Jesus faced extreme temptation by Satan in the desert, he responded by quoting the words of God from Deuteronomy.

We must also cultivate personal prayer to our loving heavenly Father. Jesus regularly withdrew for private prayer before facing the challenges of his ministry. He warned his disciples not to engage in public prayer for show, but told them to "go into your room, close the door and pray to your Father, who is unseen" (Matthew 6 v 6). The "Lord's Prayer" was not given as a piece of liturgy for public recitation, but as a pattern for this "secret" prayer. It is a prayer that counteracts doubt, expressing confidence in God and the ultimate triumph of his kingdom, and asks for forgiveness, sustenance and protection

(Matthew 6 v 9-13). Those who follow the pattern of this prayer will strengthen their faith and protect themselves against the assaults of doubt.

We need to pray that God will grant us greater knowledge and understanding, so that we can know him better. We need more spiritual insight and wisdom to understand our world, our experiences and our emotions properly. This was a major focus of Paul's prayers for his churches. He prayed this because he wanted them to stand firm in their faith (Ephesians 1 v 17-19).

In the past Christians considered it essential to develop a daily habit of personal Bible reading and private prayer. When this is neglected, the result is likely to be a less confident faith that is more vulnerable to doubt.

Belong to a supportive church family

Although Christians are saved as individuals, our salvation brings us into relationship with God and the rest of his people. We become members of Jesus' body, the church. We don't just gain new life but also a new family. We are meant to express our relationship with our new spiritual brothers and sisters in the context of a local church, where we meet together to encourage and support each other in our faith.

The author of Hebrews urged his readers not to return to Judaism. He commanded them to pay more careful attention to the word of God, but also to support and encourage each other:

Let us hold unswervingly to the hope we profess, for he who promised is faithful. And let us consider how we may spur one another on towards love and good deeds, not giving up meeting together, as some are in the habit of doing, but encouraging one another—and all the more as you see the Day approaching. *Hebrews 10 v 23-25*

It is essential that we belong to a church family where the Bible is believed, read, taught and obeyed. The good news of the gospel should be declared and confessed at every gathering, regularly remembered at the Lord's Supper, and applied to every area of life. As we sing together, we respond emotionally to the great truths of the gospel; and as we pray together, we remember that we are all children of the same heavenly Father.

We ought to leave our church gatherings with a more confident faith. If we withdraw from church and fail to meet regularly with our brothers and sisters to hear God's word, it is inevitable that we will listen instead to the world around us or to our own emotions, with the result that we become vulnerable to doubt.

However, we also have a responsibility to *remind each other* of the gospel. Paul commanded the Christians in Colossae to:

Let the message of Christ dwell among you richly as you teach and admonish one another with all wisdom through psalms, hymns and songs from the Spirit, singing to God with gratitude in your hearts. *Colossians 3 v 16*

Whenever we gather with fellow believers, we ought to try to encourage each other in the faith. We need to speak the gospel to each other to dispel doubt and deepen assurance. All too often our conversation with each other before or after church, or at our small groups, is about irrelevant trivia rather than encouraging one another in the faith.

Allow suffering to produce maturity

One of the main causes of doubt for Christians is the suffering they or others have to endure. An experience of suffering may cause them to question the love, goodness, or even the existence of God. But the New Testament urges us to see suffering as an opportunity for *growth* in faith, rather than an evil that produces doubt. Suffering exposes our sinful self-sufficiency when we should depend on God. It forces us to have a deeper trust in him because we cannot save ourselves from harm. As Abraham, Jacob, Moses, David, Job, Jonah, and Paul experienced, God providentially uses our sufferings to refine our faith. Even Jesus "learned obedience from what he suffered" (Hebrews 5 v 8).

Paul therefore encouraged the Christians in Rome to appreciate the positive spiritual blessings of suffering:

> Therefore, since we have been justified through
> faith, we have peace with God through our Lord
> Jesus Christ, through whom we have gained
> access by faith into this grace in which we now
> stand. And we boast in the hope of the glory of
> God. Not only so, but we also glory in our suffer-

ings, because we know that suffering produces perseverance; perseverance, character; and character, hope.   *Romans 5 v 1-4*

He wrote from his personal experience of repeated suffering for the sake of the gospel, and enduring a "thorn in [his] flesh" which had taught him that the grace of God was sufficient. Peter likewise wrote that enduring trials would result in a faith that has been refined and proved genuine (1 Peter 1 v 6-9).

It is often the Christians who have suffered most who have the greatest assurance and confidence in God, because they have tasted and experienced the goodness and faithfulness of God. Those who have suffered very little are often troubled by relatively trivial doubts.

It is essential that Christians help and comfort each other as they experience suffering, reminding one another of the hope of the gospel and taking care of any practical needs. The author of Hebrews reminds his readers that they had "stood side by side" with those who were suffering insult and persecution and "suffered along with those in prison" (Hebrews 10 v 33-34). He urges them to "continue to remember those in prison as if you were together with them in prison, and those who are ill-treated as if you yourselves were suffering" (Hebrews 13 v 3).

Churches need to bring the hope and comfort of the gospel to those who are suffering, and to empathise with the pain and grief that they are feeling. As Paul said in Romans 12 v 15, we need to "rejoice with those who rejoice; mourn with those who mourn". All too often we don't know what to say to those who are suffering, and we don't know how to respond as a community. Our prayers and platitudes seem trite and unreal, and do not bring true comfort. Our awkwardness can mean that our churches only ever celebrate the blessings that people experience, with the result that they are relentlessly upbeat and unreal. The Bible never ignores the real pain caused by suffering, and records numerous examples of God's people lamenting together over the griefs of living in a fallen world that is still subject to God's judgment.

Remember God's work in history and your life

Another important way of preventing doubt is to remember all that God has done for us in the past. We are more susceptible to doubt if we cannot see God's work in the present and we have forgotten all that he has done. God repeatedly commands his people to remember what he has done for them in the past. He ordered the Israelites to celebrate the Sabbath each week, and the Passover each year, to remember how he had redeemed them from Egypt. Many of the psalms also celebrate the exodus, or God's victories over Israel's enemies. David sings of how God delivered him from the Philistines and of the forgiveness he received for his sin with Bathsheba.

Jesus commanded his disciples to remember his atoning death by celebrating the Lord's Supper together. This memorial meal is a corporate reminder of the new covenant ratified by Jesus' blood (1 Corinthians 11). It is meant to be a joyful celebration of God's grace and full forgiveness, which brings great assurance of faith. Tragically, in many churches it has become a cause of doubt as Christians are urged to morbid introspection and self-examination to see if they are "worthy" to share the supper, rather than being urged to look to Christ and rejoice in his grace.

We should also remember the ways in which God has been at work in our lives. The New Testament expects Christians to remember their conversion and their baptism. They are to remember how they used to live in wickedness and sin, and how they have been changed. They are to testify to the ways in which they have known God's grace, provision and protection.

We are especially prone to attacks of doubt when our spiritual life seems dry or uneventful, so it can be immensely helpful to remember those times when we have known the closeness, presence and power of the Lord. We can look back and celebrate his work in our lives, and trust in his promises to us. Many Christians find it helpful to keep a "spiritual journal" to record the ways they have seen God at work in their lives.

Watch for the work of God in the lives of others

We also need to be attentive to the ways God is at work in our present experience. We should not assume that he only works in dramatic or miraculous ways. We need to learn that "everyday miracles", such as patient endurance and perseverance in faith, are also works of God and signs of his reality.

The New Testament letters almost invariably begin by pointing to the way God is at work in the Christians he is writing to. The letters give praise and thanks for the faith, love, joy, growth in spiritual maturity and Christian character, or perseverance in the face of persecution show by these new believers. Paul was greatly encouraged, for example, by the news he received from Timothy's visit to Thessalonica:

> But Timothy has just now come to us from you and has brought good news about your faith and love. He has told us that you always have pleasant memories of us and that you long to see us, just as we also long to see you. Therefore, brothers and sisters, in all our distress and persecution we were encouraged about you because of your faith. For now we really live, since you are standing firm in the Lord.   *1 Thessalonians 3 v 6-8*

Often we cannot see the evidence of God's grace in our lives, whereas it might be obvious to others who have seen us change and grow. We should expect to see the glory of God in each other as we are transformed ever more into the likeness of Jesus (2 Corinthians 3 v 18). We need to open our eyes to the work of God by his Spirit through the gospel that is all around us. As we pay attention to what is happening, and hear news of what God is doing in other churches and other places, our faith and confidence will be strengthened and we will be more resilient to the danger of doubt.

Step out in faith and service

Finally, we need to remember that faith is not something just to be protected and preserved from threats and challenges. True faith is not just intellectual belief in a set of propositions, but a life of sacrificial, costly and risky obedience to the Lord Jesus. If we do nothing for Jesus out of fear of succumbing to doubt, our faith will weaken and wither, like muscles that are not put to use. Our faith will be strengthened by stepping out to serve Jesus, as we experience his power to enable us to do what might have seemed difficult or impossible (see Philemon v 6).

This is often the case in evangelism. If we are afraid to speak about Jesus because of fear of what others might think of us, or of the consequences we might face, then we will *never* experience the work of the Spirit giving us the words to speak and the confidence to speak them. But if we determine not to be ashamed of the gospel and take the risk of speaking out, we will experience God's power and presence.

It is an important principle of the Christian life that God only gives us the grace that we need for the situation we are in. We will never know the boldness that God's gives his people through his Spirit unless we take the step of speaking. We are not to put God deliberately to the test, but if we do step out in faith and obedience, he promises that he will meet our needs.

Evangelism is just one of many ways we can put our faith to work, and when we do, we should expect that our faith will grow and our assurance increase. Paul commanded Timothy to appoint faithful leaders to serve in the church in Ephesus. This would be a tough task because the church was suffering considerable difficulty.

Paul encouraged suitably qualified men and women to serve by pointing to the blessings they would gain:

> Those who have served well gain an excellent
> standing and great assurance in their faith in
> Christ Jesus.   *1 Timothy 3 v 13*

Faith that is mollycoddled and protected from risk will be weak and vulnerable. We need to act on our faith. If we do this, we will gain a greater assurance that will protect us from the onslaughts of doubt.

Are you strengthening your faith?

Perhaps you are reading this book because you are struggling with issues of doubt or a lack of confident assurance. I pray that it has helped you to find a way forward to address and resolve your problems. However, we will only be able to overcome doubt and develop a more secure and resilient faith if we observe these spiritual disciplines. Is it possible that you are struggling with doubt because you have neglected the disciplines that are vital to spiritual health and confidence? Are you:

- maintaining your personal walk with God?

- participating in a supportive church family?

- allowing suffering to produce maturity?

- remembering God's work in history and in your life?

- rejoicing to see God at work in the lives of others?

- stepping out in faith to serve Jesus?

If you are neglecting these things, then it is not surprising if you struggle with doubt or lack assurance. Putting these disciplines into practice will not guarantee freedom from doubts, but they will enable you to put your doubts into proper perspective and to help you to ensure that they do not become unbelief.

If God is the one who gives faith, why do I still have doubts?

In many ways this is an identical question to: "If God saves me from sin, why do I still have to struggle with temptation?" or: "If God rescues me from death, why do I still have to suffer in this life?"

The answer is that we live in a fallen world, which is under God's curse and judgment, and subject to the spiritual power of Satan. God does everything that is necessary to rescue us for eternity in his new creation, but we still have to struggle now against the effects of the fall. God grants us sufficient faith to be saved and receive the gift of eternal life, but we are responsible for resisting the lies of the world that seek to undermine our faith.

God has a good purpose in the doubts that he allows us to experience. They may be a test to refine and strengthen our faith, or to humble us from thinking that we are better than others who struggle with doubts, or to prepare and equip us to minister to others experiencing doubts. God promises that if we are truly his, he will protect our faith so that we will not be lost but will die trusting in Christ.

From doubt to faith

We have considered why Christians experience doubt, and what they might do to gain assurance and develop a more confident and resilient faith. I hope that what you have read has helped you to tackle your own doubts and uncertainties, and has also equipped you to help others who are struggling with doubt.

We began this book with a number of individuals who were troubled by doubt. Before you read any further, go back and read their stories again (see pages 7-10). Given what you have read in this book, can you work out the answers to these questions:

■ *Why are they suffering with doubt?*

■ *How would you help them to work through their difficulties?*

Aidan

Aidan doubts that he is really a believer because of his ongoing struggle with sexual temptation, which repeatedly causes him to lapse into the sin of looking at pornography. He needs to know that the normal Christian life is a permanent battle between the Spirit dwelling in us and our fallen, sinful flesh. He needs reassurance that his longing to resist this temptation, the victory that he enjoys over it for much of the time, and his heartfelt repentance when he falls, are positive indications of true faith in Christ. He needs to be reminded that Christ died for all of his sin—past, present and future—and that he has been fully forgiven. He needs to be encouraged to seek help from his church, and to put in place appropriate and personal accountability.

Barbara

Barbara is struggling in her faith because of her illness. She feels a sense of injustice that God is allowing her to suffer after so many years of faithful service. She needs to be reassured that these feelings are entirely natural. She needs help to understand afresh that suffering, frailty, sickness and death are an inevitable part of our human experience in a fallen world. She needs to know that God is sovereign, good and loving, and that our hope is to be with Jesus, whether he heals or not. He will grant her the grace she needs to face whatever comes. Her illness may be a wonderful opportunity to testify about God.

Catherine

Catherine is being challenged in her faith by her attraction to her new colleague, compounded by her resentment towards God because of her singleness. She is in danger of being ruled by her emotions rather than listening to what God says in his word. She needs to be convinced again, both intellectually and emotionally, that Jesus is unique, so Islam and Christianity cannot both be true. She faces a choice between a relationship with this man and her relationship with Jesus. She needs to be encouraged to find true contentment in God and trust his good plans for her.

Dan

Dan is struggling with intellectual doubts that have been prompted by exposure to arguments which he had never had to consider before. He needs to find the best Christian responses to these arguments. He needs to be part of a church where challenges to the faith are taken seriously and countered. These doubts offer an opportunity to grow in understanding, so that he will be even more confident of the truth of the Bible.

Ellie

Ellie is struggling with reconciling her love for her brother with the teaching of the Bible that homosexual activity is sinful and wrong. She is emotionally torn and tempted to reject God because he seems to be harsh and unloving. She needs to be reassured that God's commands about sexual relationships are loving and good. God does not want to stop her brother finding happiness, but rather, to enable him to find true happiness and blessing. She needs to see that her brother's main problem is not that he is gay, but that he does not know Jesus. She is not called to condemn her brother, but lovingly to point him to Jesus.

Femi

Femi is struggling because his current experience of God is not as dramatic as it was at the time of his conversion. He needs to be reassured that this is perfectly normal. He needs to understand what the Bible teaches about the everyday Christian life. Is he reading the Bible and praying? Is he still struggling against sin? He needs to be encouraged to start meeting with God's people again.

Graham

Graham is struggling with the fact that he has never had to make a positive choice to believe and trust in Jesus. He needs to be encouraged not to put too much weight on these doubts that occasionally trouble him. He may be overly introspective and temperamentally anxious. He needs to remember the ways God has been at work in him over the years, reflecting on the spiritual experiences he has enjoyed, times of assurance and the ways in which he has grown in godliness. How is God working in his life at the moment? These sporadic doubts may be a crucial opportunity to make sure his faith is his own. He will need to make a choice whether to continue to believe or whether to abandon the pretence of belief.

Jennifer

Jennifer's doubts stem from the fact that she has never had what she thinks is a valid "conversion experience". She needs to know that this is not necessary, and that she is showing all the signs of true conversion. She may be someone who is temperamentally less given to strong emotions and experiences. Does she have deep passions about other interests in her life, or might it be that her spiritual feelings are in line with her feelings about other things that are important to her? She needs to stop comparing herself unhelpfully with others.

The doubts that these professing believers are experiencing need to be taken seriously and met with loving understanding. They may not be resolved easily or quickly, and they should not be put under unhelpful pressure to get sorted. Overcoming deep-rooted doubts will take time. They each need loving Christian friends, and a loving church community, to counsel them with the word of God and pray for them.

It is, of course, possible that their doubts may ultimately lead them to fall away from the faith. If this happens, it will show that they were never true believers in the first place, and their friends and church family will need to work and pray for their genuine conversion. However, in God's mercy they can emerge from this period of doubt with their faith strengthened through the testing it has endured, able to testify to the faithfulness of God and better equipped to help others struggling with doubt.

"Faith, like health, is best maintained by growth, nourishment and exercise and not by fighting sickness. Sickness may be the absence of health, but health is more than the absence of sickness, so prevention is better than cure. Equally, faith grows and flourishes when it is well nourished and exercised, so the best way to resist doubt is to build up faith rather than simply to fight against doubt."

Os Guinness

Some resources to help with specific doubts

Science and God
John Lennox *God's Undertaker* (Lion, 2009)
Kirsten Birkett *Unnatural enemies* (Matthias Media, 1997)

History
John Dickson *Investigating Jesus: A Historian's Quest* (Lion Hudson, 2010)

Suffering
John Dickson *If I were God I'd end all the pain* (Matthias Media, 2001)

Homosexuality
Sam Allberry *Is God anti-gay?* (The Good Book Company, 2013)

The Bible
Amy Orr-Ewing *Why Trust the Bible: Answers to 10 tough questions* (IVP, 2008)

Barry Cooper *Can we really trust the Bible?* (The Good Book Company, 2014)

Truth
Andrew Wilson *If God, then what?* (IVP, 2012)

Other questions
Barry Cooper and Paul Williams *If you could ask God one question.* (The Good Book Company, 2007)

Michael Jensen *Is forgiveness really free?* (TGBC, 2014)

Bill Edgar *You asked: Your questions. God's answers* (CFP, 2013)

thegoodbook
COMPANY
Opening up the Bible

At The Good Book Company, we are dedicated to helping Christians and local churches grow. We believe that God's growth process always starts with hearing clearly what he has said to us through his timeless word—the Bible.

Ever since we opened our doors in 1991, we have been striving to produce resources that honour God in the way the Bible is used. We have grown to become an international provider of user-friendly resources to the Christian community, with believers of all backgrounds and denominations using our Bible studies, books, evangelistic resources, DVD-based courses and training events.

We want to equip ordinary Christians to live for Christ day by day, and churches to grow in their knowledge of God, their love for one another, and the effectiveness of their outreach.

Call us for a discussion of your needs or visit one of our local websites for more information on the resources and services we provide.

UK & Europe: www.thegoodbook.co.uk
North America: www.thegoodbook.com
Australia: www.thegoodbook.com.au
New Zealand: www.thegoodbook.co.nz

UK & Europe: 0333 123 0880
North America: 866 244 2165
Australia: (02) 6100 4211
New Zealand: (+64) 3 343 1990